ISBN 978-1-365-94116-0

This book is available on www.lulu.com and www.amazon.com or by direct request to the author.

To contact the author regarding permissions, speaking engagements, etc.
email LoisSzymanski@hotmail.com

Printed in the United States of America

Other Books by Lois Szymanski:
****

Surfer Dude
Wild Colt
The True Story of Sea Feather
The True Story of Miracle Man
The True Story of Quintilius
Chincoteague Ponies: Untold Tales
Out of the Sea: Today's Chincoteague Pony

Thank you to Foca.tk, Clker.com and OpenClipArt.org.

This book is dedicated to my favorite pony lover, my beautiful daughter, Shannon Meyers and to her first Chincoteague Pony, Sea Feather. Shannon has shared my love of these ponies since she was old enough to say "Chincoteague Pony."

Your Chincoteague Pony

Foal's First Year

Feeding, Health Care, Training & More

by

Lois Szymanski

To Shannon & Ellen –
Congratulations on your new adventure with Randy's gorgeous colt!
Wild Pony Wishes from Lois Szymanski

CHAPTER ONE

Your Pony Comes Home

Congratulations! You are the owner of a very special foal! Chincoteague Ponies are known to be healthy, even tempered, easy-keepers, but taking home and training a wild pony foal still takes dedication, love and patience. Just like humans, each pony will have a different personality and a different perspective of what you are trying to teach, but they all have incredible potential.

There are many reasons to want a Chincoteague Pony foal, but for many – just like me - the dream began after reading *Misty of Chincoteague*, Marguerite Henry's award winning book about the wild ponies that run free on Assateague Island, adjacent to Chincoteague Island.

Many times, it is children who are taking home foals, some through the Feather Fund -www.featherfund.org – a nonprofit group that awards two Chincoteague Pony foals each year to deserving children. But just as many adults come, wanting to make that childhood dream come true.

"As a little girl, I loved horses and read every book about horse and ponies available," said Teresa Hemphill of Tennessee. "I was raised by my grandparents so Misty of Chincoteague was one of my favorites and from that time forth, I always wanted to have one of my own. As a youth, I had ridden a blue-eyed gelding at the riding academy and knew that I had to have a blue-eyed colt from Chincoteague one day."

Hemphill said she finally made it to Chincoteague Island for her 2014 vacation. She fell in love with a little blue eyed colt but didn't bid because she didn't have a place to keep a pony.

"On the way home, my husband told me if I wanted to get one that I could start looking for land," she recalled.

Through online posts by Darcy and Steve Cole of DSC Photography Hemphill was able to watch the 2016 foals through photo posts. When a blue-eyed splash colt was born on April 18 to the mare, Diamond Jewel and stallion, Surfer Dude's Riptide, Hemphill knew this would be her foal.

"The auction was very emotional for me and when we won the bid for Twinkie, my dream came finally true," Hemphill said. "I now own a beautiful splash colt – [Surfer Dude's Twinkling Star] with the most amazing blue eyes. How many people can say that a childhood dream came true at the age of 52? I can!"

If you decide to make your dreams come true and you buy a foal at auction, you may want to know how to handle the first few years. That is what this book is all about.

Trailering

Your first step will be trailering your foal home. Joining a Chincoteague Pony community online through Yahoo groups, Facebook groups or other social media is a great place to make contacts, including finding a reliable hauler. The *I Love Chincoteague Ponies* Facebook page has a large number of experienced horsemen among their membership, including hundreds of Chincoteague Pony owners.

Once you make contact with a hauler, take the extra step and check their credentials. Make contact with previous clients or speak with others who know the individual and their history. You want to make sure your new foal makes it home safely and is in good care.

If you are hauling your own foal, you will need to follow the guidelines set forth by the Chincoteague Volunteer Fire Company. All trailers must have closed backs. Young foals have in the past jumped out the back of trailers with half doors. Your foal will not be tied, so make sure the inside of the trailer is safe. This means using a deep bedding of straw or sawdust and checking for sharp edges. File down or cover any sharp edges.

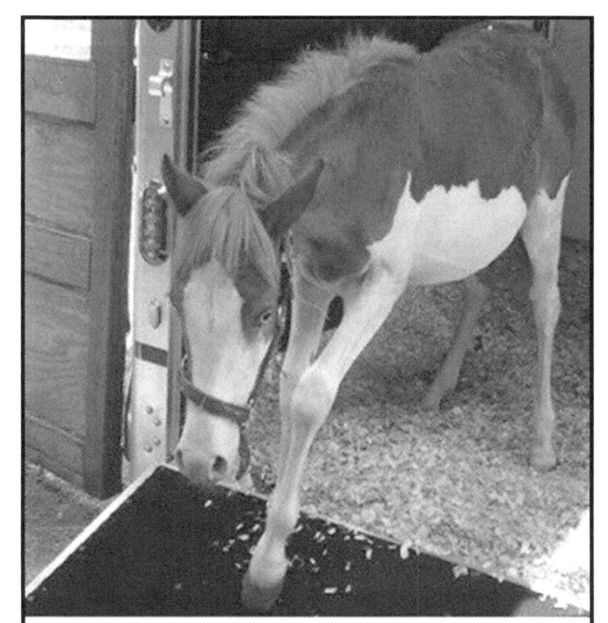

Teresa and Denny Hemphill's Chincoteague Pony foal, Surfer's Twinkling Star (Twinkie) had a long, safe ride home to Tennessee.

While in transit, your foal will need hay to munch on and fresh water. Make frequent stops to check on the foal – between 20 minutes to an hour. Depending on how long your drive is and how he settles in, you may be able to wait longer between stops later in the journey.

"I stop about every 30 minutes to check on the foals," said Debbie Roys Ober, longtime Chincoteague Pony owner and hauler and Executive Director of the Chincoteague Pony Rescue in Ridgely, Maryland. "They do well while traveling," said Ober. "I keep them on shavings in the trailer because it provides a better footing than straw, which can become slippery when they urinate. I do secure a water bucket in the trailer with the foals, since they are fearful of humans and will not drink from a hand-held bucket."

Ober said hauling more than one foal in a trailer is okay. It can actually be a source of comfort to your foal, who is leaving behind the only family he has ever known – his herd.

Ober hauled Teresa Hemphill's new foal to The Chincoteague Pony Rescue in Maryland, boarding him until Hemphill could return a few weeks later to take the colt home to Tennessee.

"We planned for the trailering by backing up the trailer and essentially creating a passage that he could walk out of his stall and into the trailer," Hemphill said. "This was Debbie Ober's idea as she is proficient in trailering foals for the Chincoteague Pony Rescue. She walked behind Twinkie and he walked out of his stall, into the passageway that we had created and up the ramp into the trailer. He stayed in the trailer overnight during our drive back to Tennessee. We stopped every hour and a half to check on him and give him water. He had a hay bag readily accessible and was fed on schedule. When we arrived home, we used the same process. We backed the trailer up, created a passage for him to walk out of trailer and into his stall with my husband walking behind him. This was a stress free way of loading and unloading for us and for Twinkie."

Stalls

The easiest way to bond with your foal is to put him inside his stall as soon as you arrive home and spend many hours inside the stall with him, building trust and letting him get to know you.

Stalls should be strong and sturdy with no sharp edges. Remove any nails, loose boards, string or any object or protrusion that could cause harm. Consider every object, even bailer twine. Horses can't throw up and have been known to choke on bailer twine, whole apples that have not been cut in pieces and other items that may appear innocent.

Alexis Dowell gave her colt, Surfer's Rogue Wave a clean, safe stall with no sharp edges, lots of room to move around and soft sawdust bedding.

A stall space of at least 10 foot by 10 foot is recommended. If two foals are sharing a stall an 8' x 12' stall works fine. Later, the pair can be separated and either of these sizes makes a great single stall. Ober said putting an older foal in a stall with a younger foal can sometimes encourage the younger one to eat and drink.

"People don't realize that the foals have no idea what a feed pan or water bucket are," Ober said. "Everything we use as normal equipment in the barn, has to be introduced to the foals."

However, when foals are kept in pairs it can take longer to bond. The foals learn to depend on each other instead of trusting their new owner.

If the barn has a concrete floor, cover the floor with rubber mats before putting down bedding. Rubber mats prevent chipping and cracking of hooves and make a hard surface more amenable. Whether the stall has a dirt floor (with or without rubber mats) or you're using rubber mats over concrete you will still need to cover the stall floor with a thick bedding of straw or sawdust.

To prevent accidents, remove halters when you are not with your foal.

To prevent tragic accidents, only use breakaway halters. These halters have a leather piece attached to the headstall or cheek sections of their halter. If the horse or foal catches the halter on something, this piece will break. Many horses – while wearing halters without the breakaway piece - have sustained serious injuries in the panic that ensues after they catch their halter. If you aren't sure if the halter you plan to use is a breakaway halter, ask a professional.

Remember to keep stalls clean and dry. Moisture promotes disease-causing bacteria and provides a breeding ground for insects. Bugs are not only an irritation - they carry a long list of infectious diseases.

CHAPTER TWO

Basic Feeding and Grooming

If your new baby is younger than five months old, special feeds for foals can help them bridge the gap between their mother's milk and a new world of grass, hay and commercial pony feed. Tribute brand Growth Textured feed, Mare and Foal feed by Nutrena and Omolene 300 Foal Formula are highly recommended.

Whenever you are feeding or offering treats always use a feed pan or bucket to prevent nipping, which often starts when a foal associates your hand with treats. Your horse is a valued investment and a future friend and you want to keep him or her healthy and growing at a steady pace.

Ruth Provost spoke of the reason she and her daughter, Josette chose to purchase their colt out of the mare Diamond Jewel and by the stallion Courtney's Boy, why they named it Josie's Boy, and why his call name is Journey.

"We wanted to honor the very first horse we started this adventure with and that we lost very suddenly. His name was Joey," she said. "And we wanted to have a part of Courtney's Boy's name included. I always figured someone named Courtney's Boy after a daughter or wife. My daughter's name is Josette. She and I started this quest together in 2008. Josette liked how [Journey] started with Jo and ended with ey, like our Joey and we nicknamed him Journey because this has been our journey together."

Josette Provost-Kosko feeds a treat to her Chincoteague Pony colt, Josie's Boy - nicknamed Journey. He's come to trust her and look for his treat.

Sometimes you just know when a foal belongs with you. That's why Ruth and her daughter did not give up when the bidding soared to an incredibly high price. In the months leading up to Pony Penning they had watched this foal through pictures and posts on Facebook.

"We do not know how we could ever have left that auction without him," Ruth said. "We just could not let him go."

Just like Journey, your new foal is a valuable addition to your family. Good feed creates a foundation for his future. When feeding the first time, watch for choking. Some do fine. Others do not. You can soak a cup of feed with a half of quart of warm water to soften it. Your vet may also recommend a milk replacer.

Debbie Ober at the Chincoteague Pony Rescue uses Tribute feeds.

"My Tribute distributor recommends foals stay on the Tribute Foal Foundation until they are six months of age," Ober said. "At that time, you can change to the Tribute Growth, which comes in a textured or pellet formulas. They can stay on that until they reach two years of age."

Ober said she doesn't use sweet feeds, which have a high starch and sugar content that she feels promotes hyperactivity in equines.

"The Tribute products are complete feeds, so no added expense is needed for supplements or milk powders and/or pellets," she said. "Once you change to the Tribute Growth feed, you can add these if you want, but it's not necessary. "

Ober doesn't use Mare and Foal feeds which she says are high in sugars, although several brands do offer a low starch variety.

"I have one yearling who chokes on pellets," Ober said, "so I have all our yearling fillies on the textured feed."

Teresa Hemphill said she switched Twinkie from Tribute Foal Foundation feed to Tribute Growth Formula when he was about five months old by mixing his feed - with 1/3 being the new feed.

Offer mold-free, quality grass hay when fresh grass is not readily available. Chincoteague Ponies seldom need higher grade hays and can gain weight fast. Do not feed dusty or moldy hay.

An important note – NEVER throw cut grass over the fence for your horse to eat. Feeding lawn clippings upsets the balance of microbes in the hindgut and can lead to colic – which can be fatal, or laminitis – which can cripple a horse.

It is important to note that the minute grass is cut it enters a fermentation stage that produces dangerously high fermentable and harmful carbo-hydrates. This is why cut grass retains heat and hay is cured in the sun before use.

As he transitions from mare's milk to a new feed and water regimen, your foal also needs plenty of fresh, clean drinking water in a bucket or trough that is cleaned regularly.

Grooming

Grooming your horse is important. A clean horse feels more comfortable and is less likely to develop skin conditions. Plus, it helps your foal get used to being handled, right from the start.

You should keep your grooming supplies handy in a wide bucket or a grooming tray that should contain a curry comb or grooming mitt, a body brush with slightly stiffer bristles, a fine, soft bristled brush for finishing, a plastic mane and tail comb (because there is less breakage than with metal), a soft

Alexis Meyers grooms her mom's Chincoteague Pony, Sea Feather.

sponge – or clean, soft cloth, and a hoof pick. It is also nice to have scissors, or later on – clippers.

I always start with the curry comb, although some use a curry mitt. This is designed to loosen the dirt in the coat. Using a circular motion, go over the entire body, loosening up dust and dead hair as you go. Be gentle on the hips, neck and shoulders. If your horse has sensitive skin he will let you know with his reactions – by switching his tail or laying back his ears, stomping or swinging his head - and you can use less pressure.

While you work, be mindful of any bumps from fly bites, open sores or anything out of the ordinary. If there is a problem, use your first aid kit to treat or call a vet if necessary.

After currying the body with a mitt or coarse brush to loosen and wipe away caked dirt, go to work with the body brush to sweep away what you have missed. With extensive strokes, follow the direction of the hair growth, working your way around the foal or horse. I also use this brush to do the legs because it is a softer brush.

The finishing brush, with shorter, softer bristles works best for your pony's face. Work with short, soft, gentle strokes. Afterward, use a damp sponge or soft cloth to wipe around the horse's eyes and muzzle. Check your pony's eyes to be sure there is no redness, or swelling. Eye infections should be treated promptly.

You can also apply fly spray or sun screen at this time, if necessary. Now, it is on to the mane and tail. Use the mane and tail brush to carefully detangle long hair in the mane and tail. I sometimes use a curry comb to start the untangling process. When brushing the tail, stand to one side and pull the tail gently over to you so you are not in line for a kick. You can't rule out a stray kick with even the gentlest horse if they are agitated by flies or startled. Commercial grooming sprays and detanglers can help if there are burrs or exceptionally bad tangles.

Don't forget to clean the hooves, which may be more important than the body. Use the hoof pick to pry out any dirt, manure or anything else lodged in the frog or sole of the foot. The smell is always horrible but if it changes to something putrid you may need to rule out thrush, a stinky hoof disease that is easily treated but should never be let go. Check for cracks in the wall of the hooves before finishing.

Some folks use hoof oils or ointments. They do make the hooves look nice but their usefulness is debated. Some believe it prevents the hoof from absorbing necessary moisture while others feel it seals in moisture.

CHAPTER THREE

Health Care

Your foal is home! He's in the stall, waiting for you. While you sit quietly, waiting for trust to grow between you and your new baby, take time to learn about his upcoming health care needs.

Health Care Visits

Just about every filly and colt that leaves the island will need immediate worming. Worms and worm larvae are often pulled up on the root of the very grasses they need to ingest. Some say that no horse is ever completely worm-free. Chincoteague Ponies are known to start their lives with a pack full of worms onboard. When a horse defecates, worms and worm larvae are passed through his body, re-infecting the soil where they eat.

Worms can seriously impact an equine life, so every effort must be made to keep them under control. Manure holds worms and larvae and must not be allowed to accumulate around stables, shelters and pastures. In small pastures or enclosures manure should be hauled out weekly.

There are many kind of worms – round worms, blood worms, tapeworms, pinworms, bots and more. Because no single wormer is effective against all types and/or stages of worms, rotating brands of worm medicine is recommended.

Deb Ober at the Chincoteague Pony Rescue said as soon as she can handle a new foal she begins worming bi-weekly.

"The first two wormings [are given] at half the required dose for their weight," Ober said, adding that foals just off the island are loaded with worms. "This gives them two chances to get rid of many worms before hitting them with a stronger dose. I use [the brand] Safeguard for the first worming, then Strongid for the second [dose - two weeks later]. The third worming is a full dose for their weight with the Safeguard Paste."

Ober said new foal owners should allow two weeks between each half dose.

"A foal can colic and die if too strong of a dose is used from the start," she warned. "After the third worming, I wait four weeks, then give the Strongid Paste again in the full dosage for the foal's weight."

After the fourth dose, Ober goes to monthly doses of worm paste, rotating the brand of worm paste as suggested by her vet.

Vaccines

Most states require a negative Coggins test be onboard the trailer for any horse crossing a state line, but in many states foals are an exception. Chincoteague Pony foals all leave pony penning with paperwork that shows their herd has been tested and has a negative Coggins rating.

Just like human babies, foals need to be vaccinated against deadly equine diseases. At birth, the foal inherits disease protection from his dam through the colostrum he gets in his first stages of nursing. Whatever vaccines the herd has received travel to him via his dam. But eventually those maternal antibodies dissipate and proper immunization is a must.

Veterinarian and Chincoteague Pony owner, Allison Dotzel said when her Chincoteague Pony, Finn was a foal she followed the recommendations of the American Association for Equine Practitioners.

Veterinarian, Allison Dotzel's 2015 colt, Finn with his new friend, Sammy Harvey.

"They are our biggest professional organization of equine veterinarians," Dotzel said, "and [they] put out a lot of research in all areas of equine medicine so I consider them a pretty reliable source."

Dotzel spoke of the immunities your foal will come with.

"The Chincoteague Volunteer Fire Company gives Eastern Encephalomyelitis/Western Encephalomyelitis, West Nile Virus, Tetanus and Rabies to the herd so the foals will have maternal immunity for those diseases," she said. 'This immunity lasts at least three to four months and up to six months.

Vaccinations are available on the carnival grounds by the fire company veterinarian at Pony Penning. Although many people do get their foal's shots before departing from Pony Penning, Ober says she does not use the fire department's veterinary services.

"Because most are only three months old and many are younger, I never vaccinate at the carnival grounds," she said. "They are under too much stress as it is, so why make it harder on them?"

Deb Ober holds Bristol, who came to the Chincoteague Pony Rescue as a one day old foal. As a 4-year-old, the mare has been doing round pen work and has been tacked up, but won't be ridden for a while. There's plenty of ground work and desensitization to do first," Ober said.

Ober said her veterinarian recommends starting vaccines at four months of age.

"We break it up into two farm calls to vaccinate," she said. "The young foals get the same dose as a large horse so it can be too much on their system at one visit."

Ober said her vet gives no shots until five to six months including a five-way shot for Eastern/ Western Encephalomyelitis, flu, Rhino, Tetanus and West Nile.

"Eastern Western/Tetanus/West Nile can be started at four to six months and boosted four to six weeks later," Dotzel said of the core shots all foals should receive. "Rabies [are] given at six months and boosted four to six weeks later. Those are the vaccines that the AAEP considers to be core vaccines and should be given to all foals regardless of their geographic area and environment."

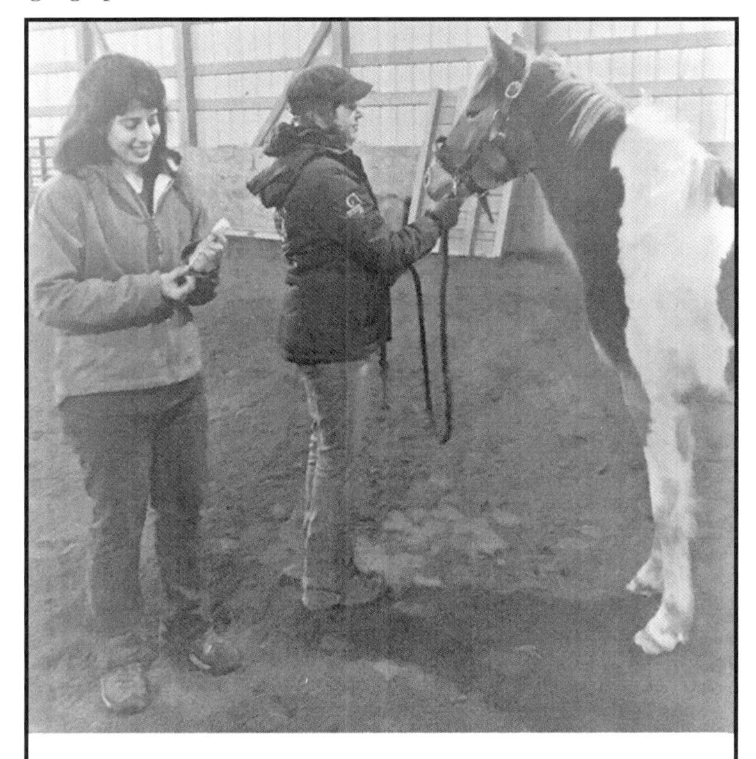

Veterinarian, Allison Dotzel loads a needle for shots while trainer, Tipson Myers holds Chincoteague Pony, Finn.

Non-core vaccines that Dotzel said she considers to be important are Botulism, Potomac Horse Fever, Equine Herpes Virus (EVH), and Equine Influenza.

"Botulism occurs most commonly with wet, swampy pastures and in horses that eat round bales," Dotzel said. "It is not very common in my area of Pennsylvania and I don't use this vaccine a lot for my patients. However, it can be a devastating disease and it is probably a good one to give especially in the Mid-Atlantic region and South Eastern United States."

Dotzel said Chincoteague Pony foals have no maternal immunity for Botulism, so a first dose should be at one to three months of age with two boosters at four and eight weeks after initial vaccination.

The AAEP recommends starting Potomac vaccine at five months but it can be started earlier in high risk areas. If started early, boosters should be given every four weeks until the foal is six months old. This one is very important in the mid-Atlantic area," she said.

According to Dotzel, both EHV and Equine Flu can be started at four to six months of age and boosted four to six weeks later.

"These are a good idea for babies in general, especially if they will be traveling to shows or around other horses that travel," Dotzel said. "For Strangles, most people use the modified live vaccine and that should be started at six to nine months of age and boosted three to four weeks later. This disease can be nasty, particularly for young and old horses so it's a good idea for people who have their foals at barns where other horses are coming and going. People who have closed herds where horses never come and go might not need this one.

Like Ober, Dotzel said there is no reason to vaccinate until after your foal arrives home.

"Except for botulism, these foals really don't need to have any vaccines until at least four months of age which is why I don't like the idea of vaccinating them at the auction. I feel it stresses them unnecessarily and really doesn't help them. I would recommend that they get the foal home and settled for two to three weeks before giving [any shots]," Dotzel said.

Find the schedule of shots on the web site:

http://www.aaep.org/custdocs/FoalVaccinationChart.pdf

Especially while your foal is young, it is best to err on the side of caution. If your foal is sick, call a vet. Do not try to self-diagnose. Even a small thing can be a big deal, as Chincoteague Pony owner, Nathan Turell will attest.

The 2008 Chincoteague Pony foal that Nathan took home to New York, with help from the Feather Fund, developed a life-threatening case of Strangles, and only thru his diligent actions and with the help of Cornell University's Equine Center did his gelding, Eleazar's Feather survive.

Nathan was 13 and dreaming of becoming a vet one day, a goal he is now

Nathan Turrell, outside the isolation shelter he and his family built for his Chincoteague Pony, Eleazar's Feather, after the pony contracted Strangles.

pursuing in college. He says he will never forget that May afternoon that his two-year-old old pony began a journey for survival. He had just arrived at the barn where he boarded his pony. Unbeknownst to him, another pony at the barn had not been vaccinated for Strangles and was carrying the virus.

"My pony seemed depressed, uninterested in food, disinterested in water. I thought, *Colic, I better called the vet.* What my pony experienced is something I feel should be shared with all horse owners," Turrell said.

After two visits from the vet, a rectal exam and IV fluids, Turrell said Eleazar was transported to Cornell University's equine medical facility.

"His colon was twisted and surgery was inevitable," Turrell said. "When we arrived at Cornell, surprisingly, his colon had untwisted, but something was still not right so he was kept for observation."

Throughout the night, a battle raged in Eleazar's young body. His vital signs worsened, his fever peaked to 106.8, and the glands under his jaw swelled rapidly. Strangles was diagnosed and he was immediately isolated."

Turrell said if Strangles is confirmed the pony must immediately be isolated and every precaution must be taken to keep the bacterial infection from spreading. When his pony was finally able to come home he was taken to an isolated shelter on the farm, with a small turnout area a good distance away from his father's horse, and washing and cleanup routines were strictly followed.

"I needed to monitor my pony's temperature, clean and medicate his ruptured abscesses, give him Bute for his fever, and Gastrogaurd for ulcer prevention. Since Eleazar had lost 100 pounds we needed to monitor his food and water intake, and manure output. It was helpful to keep a daily log tracking his progress," Nathan said.

Turrell said Eleazar's isolation station was set up before he arrived home.

"I made sure he had his own feed and water buckets, brushes, tack, pitchfork, and wheel barrel. As for me, I had rubber gloves, boot covers, coveralls, medical supplies, and plenty of disinfectant. My arsenal of disinfectants consisted of Novasan, chlorhexidine solution, hand sanitizer, and Clorox. I joked that we had stock in these items. Three times a day I faithfully prepared for the battle against bacteria. Armed in protective gear, I performed my daily chores. My most challenging task was making sure manure and disinfectant were disposed of safely," he said

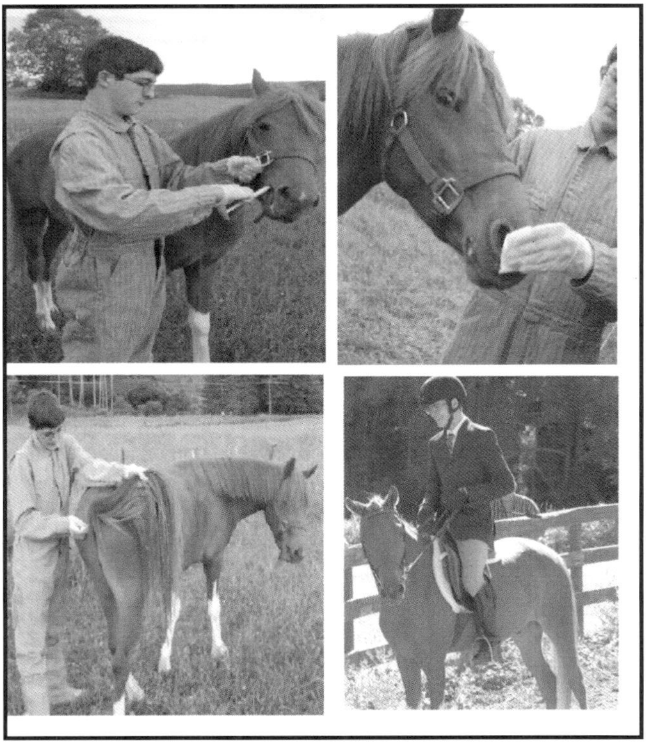

According to Turrell, anyone dealing with infectious equine diseases should also disinfect their horse trailer, stall, or any other items the pony was exposed to, before isolation."

Turrell said Strangles is not usually fatal, but it is highly contagious and can be messy, especially when abscesses rupture. Some severe complications are linked to Strangles. Thankfully, Eleazar survived and is well today.

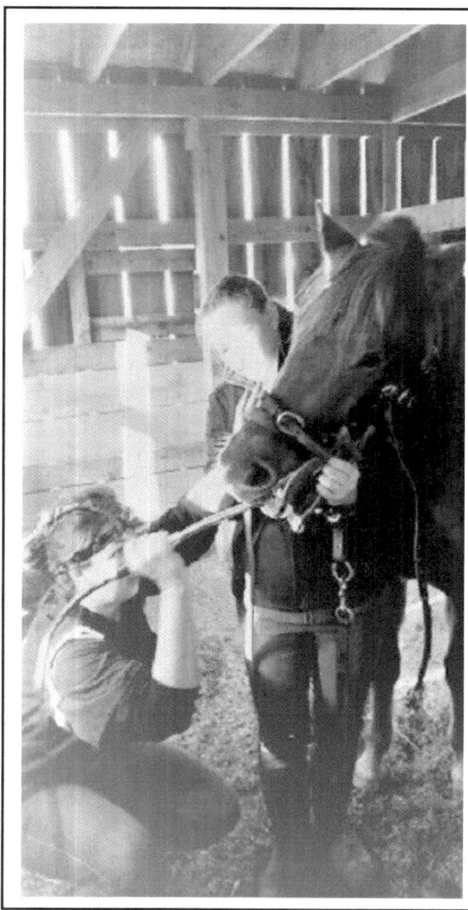

Sabrina Dobbins holds her Chincoteague Pony, Blessing while equine dentist, Lindsey Burch examines Blessing's teeth. Dobbins wanted to be sure her pony's teeth were fine before putting a bit in her mouth for the first time.

CHAPTER FOUR

Additional Health Care & Pasture Management

Dental Care

In an article in Horse Journal Magazine, veterinarian, Grant Miller said, like rabbits and cows, a horse's teeth grow continually throughout his life. Grazing and eating grain keeps them worn down.

"As the teeth grow, the repetitive circular chewing motion causes the premolars and molars (cheek teeth) to form sharp enamel points. In most cases, these sharp points form on the outside edges of the upper premolars and molars, and on the inside edges of the lower premolars and molars," Miller wrote. "Over time, sharp points can irritate the cheeks and tongue, even change the way the horse chews. Floating [a term used for filing] the teeth reduces sharp points and levels occlusal surfaces in an effort to "balance" the mouth."

Horses whose teeth are cared for can eat more comfortably, chew more efficiently and their teeth last longer, so calling an equine dentist is sometimes necessary.

Sabrina Dobbins, got her Chincoteague Pony foal, A Feather's Blessing with help from the Feather Fund in 2014. When Blessing was two years old, Dobbins had an equine dentist come to check the mare's teeth.

"I didn't notice she had any problems but I wanted to get her teeth checked out before I put a bit in her mouth," Dobbins said. "I plan to do regular visits because I'd prefer to get the mildly sharp edges floated before I see a problem such as dropping feed or losing weight.

Equine dentist, Joel Nupp agreed with Dobbins.

"Foals will have some teeth at birth," Nupp said. "Horses have what's called a hypsodont teeth. They grow in the skull until they are six years old. They are 75 mm long then and erupt at 2mm per year. I recommend all horses, regardless of use, be floated starting when they are 2 years old - or before they are ridden. I recommend yearly checkups for the life of the horse.'

Because of the groundwork they put in while their foal was very young, Ruth and Josette Provost's 2016 filly, Journey stands quietly for her first visit with the farrier.

Farrier

When you are able to pick up your foal's hooves one at a time, with ease, it is time to call the farrier. We want the farrier to be so impressed he comments on this wonderful breed, the Chincoteague Pony!

Throughout his entire life, the farrier should visit your foal every five to eight weeks, depending upon his hoof growth rate. Your farrier will monitor hoof health and will trim. Horses carry a lot of weight on those all-important hooves and they will one day carry you too, so keeping them healthy is of paramount importance.

Keeping Flies at Bay

During the days that you are thinking about vaccines and doing that first worming, also remember to protect your foal from germ-carrying flies and biting bugs with fly sprays and masks.

Veterinarian Alison Meyer said she has tried many fly products on their two Chincoteague Ponies, Cowboy and Salty. "I have tried Avon Skin So Soft, homemade sprays using citronella combinations as well as vinegar solutions. I have tried expensive commercial sprays and cheap commercial sprays and honestly, I haven't found the perfect one for my farm," Meyer said, "but I've had the most luck with Absorbine Ultra Shield products. I have also liked using the Farnam Swat Fly ointment for their legs and ears."

Meyer said one of her friends uses a commercial diary facility insect spray that is diluted and applied with a plant sprayer. Many of the people I spoke with say each horse responds differently. New pony owners should try several brands to see what works for them.

Trainer, Summer Barrick has cared for many new island foals. Her 2005 Chincoteague Pony, Starlight Blessing – a pony she took home with help from the Feather Fund - is currently making a mark in dressage arenas.

Barrick said she uses Bronco brand fly spray and Swat for the face and when the foal has a wound. "I put Swat around [the wound] so bugs stay away," she said.

Barrick said it is not hard to find fly masks for foals. She's found them at Dover Saddlery and online with Amazon.com

"I recommend [a fly mask] with ears," she said, noting that it is harder to find fly masks with ear covers for foals than it is to find them for full grown ponies and horses.

Twins, Trisha and Courtney Gagne used a fly mask with ear covers to protect their 2014 colt, Kindred Spirit.

There are several different kinds of fly masks. You will want to compare them to find the one that is right for your foal.

Pasture Management

Two acres of pasture per horse is a good measure to use when thinking of optimal pasture size, although many horses do just fine in dry lots, as long as there is room for your pony to run and kick up his heels and as long as quality hay is fed on a daily basis. In smaller lots, it is also imperative that manure be picked up on a regular basis to prevent the spread of worms and other parasites.

During the years we were raising Chincoteague Ponies and foals our smaller pasture stayed vibrant with manure by gates and standing areas picked up on a daily basis. We also picked up manure across the entire field at least every 8 to 12 days. We kept a manure wagon near the gate to pitch manure into and kept a running list of gardeners who wanted manure. Every time the wagon was full we hauled it off to gardens across our county. People laughed whenever we talked about our manure list but we truly had so many people wanting manure that we frequently got calls asking, "When can I get my load of manure?"

Having a lush green horse pasture offers natural feed for your pony, reduces the cost of feeding and provides your horse with room to exercise. Horses are healthier when they reside in a healthy pasture.

Most horses avoid eating in areas with piles of manure. They know it may well be infested with worm larvae. In addition, they don't like to eat trampled grass or weedy grass, so try to keep your pasture from being overgrazed. If you have the land available, rotating pastures is ideal. Two to three weeks between each rotation – with less during the rainy season - will give grass the growing time it needs.

Mowing is also an important part of pasture management for horses. It cuts down on the spread of weeds to produce higher quality grass. Mowing weeds before seed-heads appear helps minimize weeds. Mowing grass to a three to four inch height is optimal. The grass produced will be lower in fiber but higher in protein.

Occasional dragging of the pasture enables air and water to penetrate the soil more effectively and helps to uncover and destroy parasitic eggs and larvae that will then die in the hot sun. An effective drag can be made from a 48" welded wire cattle panel if you make sure the long wires are horizontal. You can drag this behind a four-wheeler or mower or tractor. It works well in dry lots and areas where the grass is short.

It's important to have a place where your pony can run and get proper exercise. Pasture management helps to maintain quality grass for foraging, too. Here, Caroline Butler's Chincoteague Pony, Quintillius enjoys his lush pasture.

Another way to boost your pasture is to spread good forage grass seed annually, usually in spring or fall. Don't allow grazing in this area for at least six weeks after new seed has emerged.

Again, please remember to never feed your horse grass clippings that you've raked up after mowing the yard, as they are an extreme threat.

CHAPTER FIVE

Bonding and Baby Steps

Bonding

The quickest way to bond with your foal is to keep him inside his stall until he calmly allows you to approach him, put a halter on and buckle it. Take time to earn his trust. He will be less fearful if you are patient and wait for him to approach you first – on his terms.

First time Chincoteague Pony foal owners often recommend sitting in the stall in a lawn chair or on a stool and waiting for your foal to approach you, however long it takes. Many children who have received foals from the nonprofit, The Feather Fund say they read books to their foals. The sing-song sound of reading seems to have a calming effect.

New babies are shy but they are curious by nature and will eventually approach. Hold your hand out, palm up, for him to sniff. A little feed in a bucket offers strong encouragement.

Twins, Courtney and Trisha Gagne were awarded the opportunity to choose and bid on their favorite foal at Pony Penning after they applied to the nonprofit, The Feather Fund. Courtney talked about the wait to touch their foal, Kindred Spirit.

"We did a lot of sitting and waiting with Spirit inside his pen," she said. "But after about three days we could start with hand grooming, moving to brushes next. As a baby he didn't mind anything," Courtney said.

Start with simple gentle touches. Within a short time you will be grooming your foal and he will be enjoying it. Use a soft cloth first and work your way up to soft brushes, mane and tail combs and picking out the hooves, which should be done on a regular basis.

Charity Bradford and Laura Bagley play HorseOpoly while Laura's 2016 Feather Fund foal, Tug looks on.

Laura Bagley of New York said she also used this method with her foal, Tug, spending as much time as possible with her colt, even sleeping in the stall with him during the first week and bringing friends to play games outside his stall during daytime hours. This helped him get used to the sound of human voices so he could learn to trust.

Haltering

The first official step in the training process may be getting your foal to accept a halter. Each foal is different so the timeframe for getting a halter in place differs. After talking to multiple Chincoteague Pony foal owners, it seems it can take from a few hours to a week for a foal to accept and trust his new owner enough to be haltered without fear.

The halter goes over the horse's head, is pulled up around the muzzle and over the poll and ears and is buckled beside the cheek. To get your foal used to the halter, rub it down his neck and over his back and body. Allow him opportunities to sniff the halter before applying. Remember that every-single thing in this new life is a big change from all he's known.

Make sure the halter is the right size and a good fit. A tight halter will rub hair from the face and will be uncomfortable for the foal. A loose halter could get snagged on feed buckets and stall doors and even in the foal's back hoof when he scratches his face.

When your foal is used to the rattle and feel of a halter on and around his body you can slowly slide the halter over his head and buckle it. Keep an eye on him as he gets used to the feel of his new headgear. If the fit is right it won't be long until he forgets he even has it on.

Leading

Once your horse seems comfortable wearing his halter you can begin training him to lead. Leading can be taught in a large stall or a small outside paddock. This is an important task. Whenever you need to bring your foal inside or out, onto a trailer or off, as well as throughout multiple phases of training being able to lead calmly plays a big role.

First, clip the lead line to the halter. There are many kinds of lead lines available for purchase. I like to start with a long cotton one. Standing on the left-hand side of your horse, take the lead in your right hand, holding it about a foot or two away from his chin. Fold or bunch the remaining line in your left hand. Never wrap it around your hand. If the foal were to bolt, you would be pulled along which could hurt you and could also startle the foal during his critical early training period.

Stand at your foal's left shoulder, facing in the same direction. With the lead line under his chin, apply gentle forward pressure, taking a single small step.

Keith Hosman, in his book "Your Foal: Essential Training" says learning to give in to pressure "is the fundamental concept behind all training – it's a biggie." And Hosman says, "Fighting pressure is a natural response," so expect your foal to bulk.

Keep the pressure consistent until your foal steps forward. Then immediately release the pressure, tell him he is a good boy and pat his neck. This will reward him for taking that step and he will remember that reward. If you want your foal to learn voice commands you can stay "Walk on" or make a clicking sound, a signal given in unison with the lesson.

Repeat this again and again until you find that he is taking a step as soon as you apply forward pressure. If he doesn't catch on, take a break. Hosman recommends teaching a horse to give in to pressure even before that first step. Although most of the folks I have talked to who are raising their own foals did not do this, I believe it is useful advice.

In his book, Hosman says to hold the line several inches below the foal's head and apply about two pounds of pressure toward your body. The goal is to get the foal to turn his head slightly or relax his neck. Drop the line the instant you feel even a slight relaxation, thereby rewarding the foal for turning his head toward you or relaxing the neck.

Whether you do the relaxation/head turn exercise or go straight to leading, remember to be patient.

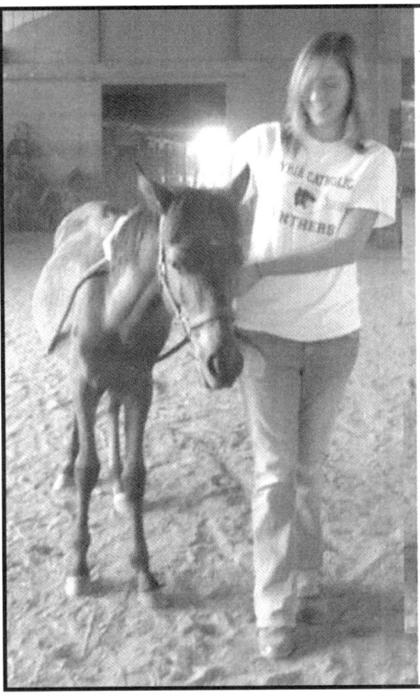

Amy Wetzel used the rump-rope method to train her 2011 colt, Babe's Buckeye to lead. Buckeye also joined Amy for 3 years at the University of Findlay and was trained through their equine program while Amy majored in equestrian studies and minored in equine business management.

Another way to help your foal learn to lead is to apply pressure to the rump with a butt rope. Using an extra-long lead rope, attach it to the halter on the foal's left side, wrap it around the left side of the body, over the rump just below the tail (never under the tail) along the right side of the body and toward the foal's head.. When you give the cue to step forward, apply gentle pressure to the left side of the halter, and use the right side as a pulley, applying pressure to his rump. The feeling for him is the same as when another horse leans against him in the field and should result in him stepping forward.

During either process, do not yank his head or try to overpower him. He's stronger than you think. Even though pulling until he is off balance may get him to take a step, it's not a step in the right direction. If your foal doesn't succumb to gentle pressure it's because he doesn't understand what you want him to do. Be patient and add extra sessions if necessary.

Chincoteague Pony owner, Amy Wetzel's pony, Babe's Buckeye was nearly a year old when she brought him home to Ohio with help from the Feather Fund in 2011.

"That first week Buckeye did not understand how to give to the pressure of the halter and wrapping the rope around his hind end really helped," Wetzel said. "I would first cue him with the halter and when he didn't respond to that I would put light pressure on the rope which he wanted to move away from, getting him to take that step that I wanted. He caught on very quickly to this and I only had to use it a few times before he started understanding the concept of leading with a halter. I found it was very important in desensitizing your pony to have a rope touch them on any part of their body. That helps with future training and saddling, too."

Never whip, hit, shove or force your foal. If you lose his trust at this young age it will be hard to regain. Also try not to work with a young foal for more than 20 minutes to a half hour at a time and try not to do more than two - half hour training sessions per day. Like a small child, he has a short attention span and will tire quickly. If you burn him out he will run *from* you instead of toward you when he anticipates another training session.

Once your foal is moving forward you can add new cues. Using a voice command he can remember like *halt*, *whoa*, or *stand* can be helpful in future training sessions as his knowledge base advances. It is also advantageous to teach your foal to stand in crossties for grooming, clipping and hoof care.

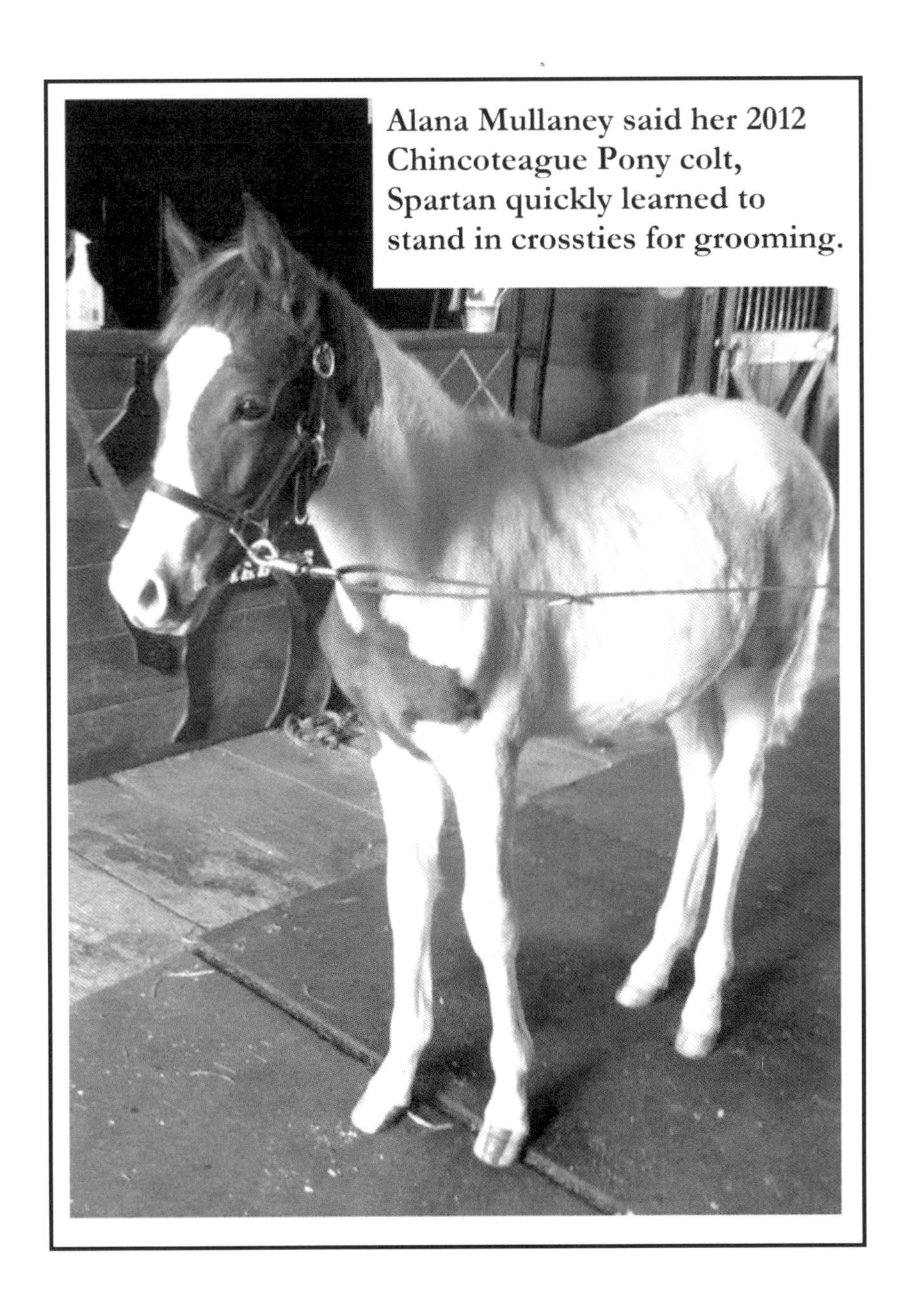

Alana Mullaney said her 2012 Chincoteague Pony colt, Spartan quickly learned to stand in crossties for grooming.

This is Veronica Webb and Miracle in the Making, the Chincoteague Pony the Feather Fund helped her purchase in 2004. This was the first foal the Feather Fund gifted in memory of their founding angel, Carollynn Suplee.

CHAPTER SIX

Outside the Stall

Your new foal is not only following your commands, he is happy to see you when you come, maybe even nickering at your approach. He has begun to enjoy your touch and stands to be groomed. You can lead him in a circle around the stall. He has earned outside time!

Now you can turn your foal out into a small paddock with supervision. Daily exercise – including bucking and racing around the paddock – helps him develop muscles. Each day, you can increase your foal's outside time a bit more until he becomes familiar with his surroundings and feels comfortable being left alone.

Herd-Mates and Meeting Others

Horses are herd animals, and while many do well on their own, it is always best to allow your horse to have a herd mate. If, having two horses is more than you can handle, other options exist. Goats, sheep and even pigs make great pasture mates.

Frequently, when a new horse is introduced to a herd there is a lot of squealing, kicking and carrying on. This is less likely to happen with a foal. Horses seem more accepting of foals. Still, there are recommended precautions.

First, it helps to put the new foal into a field next to its future herd mates and let them meet over the fence for a day or two up to a week. If you

Chincoteague Pony, Blessing and her pot-bellied pig friend, grazing together.

only have one pasture, open the top stall door and let them meet over the stall door. This gives them a chance to figure each other out and learn who is in charge.

Another recommendation comes if you have a particularly bossy alpha horse in the pasture. If this is the case, introduce the newbie to the rest of the herd while the alpha horse is stabled or in a separate pasture.

"I think slowly introducing through a fence is the best route," said Chincoteague Pony owner, Sabrina Dobbins. "Once they seem to tolerate each other through a fence introduce them together in a field."

Dobbins, who received her foal, Blessing from the Feather Fund, has spent the past few years working at a Clydesdale Farm, with foals and horses of all ages and sizes while competing in 4-H horse shows.

"For Blessing, there was a round pen in her field. I put her in the round pen for a few days to get used to the other horses. Once everything seemed ok while she was "safe" in the round pen, I put her in the big field under my supervision for the first day. Then I left her out for a few hours at a time without me. When I noticed all of them getting along, she was turned out all day with the others."

Lindsay Geiser said her Chincoteague Pony foal, Comet was bullied by the first horse he was turned out with, but now he does just fine.

Sometimes there is an issue, but there are ways to work around it. 2011 Feather Fund recipient, Lindsay Geiser said it took some time for her Chincoteague Pony, Comet to adjust.

"We had to try letting him out with a couple of different horses because the first one we tried bullied him too much," Geiser said. "After about a week of one-on-one with the second horse we tried we were able to introduce him to a small herd and eventually to the horse who bullied him. The horse he was turned out with for a week individually "adopted" him and protected him from the one who picked on him."

Geiser said no matter who Comet is out with in the field, he always runs to meet her when he sees her coming.

The horsemen and women that I spoke to said if there is going to be a blow up it usually happens within the first half hour to forty-five minutes. Keep an eye on them and remove the new foal if there is a problem. Most horses find a way to bond in time.

Outside Training

Now that your foal is spending time in the pasture, your training can continue in short outside sessions. Teach him to stand still for longer periods of time while on the lead line. And then teach him to back up. Here are some tips to get you get started.

Spending time outside with her 2004 foal, Miracle was an important part of 10-year-old Veronica Webb's training process.

First, establish a verbal cue for backing up. This can be something as simple as the word, *Back*. Standing beside your foal, bring the lead rope down, directly beneath the chin. Apply gentle, consistent pressure on the lead line until he responds by stepping back. As soon as he shifts his weight to step back - release the pressure and praise him. Pat his neck. Scratch his favorite spot. Tell him he is a good boy. Soon he'll learn that downward pressure is a cue to move backward and stepping back nets him a reward.

During the training process, it is important to pay attention to everything going on around you so you are aware and prepared for anything that could startle your foal. If he is startled and begins to buck or run, don't yank the lead line. Instead, let the line flow through your fingers and move in sync with him. Chances are that he will settle down before he reaches the end of the line. If he takes off, turn him in a circle. Moving with him, make the circle smaller and smaller until he is at your side again. Don't yell or punish him. Use quiet tones and calming words until he realizes there is no reason for fear.

One way to avoid a situation where your foal bolts or reacts in a dangerous way is to watch his body language and wait for him to relax. If his head is held sky high with ears up it is likely that he is on edge. Wait with him until he lowers his head. This loosens the spine and aids in relaxation. Use soft tones and gentle body language. Choosing and repeating the same monotone word (something like "Easy") can establish that connection to a cue that teaches him to relax when necessary. Chincoteague Pony owner, Veronica Web said, "The most important thing for new foal owners to know is patience and [that they need] to build trust. This is a pony that will take you far in life, whatever discipline you are wanting to partake in. Establishing their trust in you as a leader is crucial. They don't know what you're asking of them at first. Baby steps in all you do will make greater strides in in their training, even further down the road. Don't ask too much of them too soon, keep lessons short and sweet, and always end on a positive note. Remember, they look at you as a leader, and remember to have fun and enjoy the experience."

Patience in the Process

As you move through the stages of training remain patient with your foal, but do not allow him to get away with poor behavior. It is easy to fall into the "always be sweet and kind" mode, but you cannot let your foal be in charge. If you don't let him know that you are in control you could end up with a dangerous horse in the future.

Chincoteague Ponies are one of the most sensible breeds out there. Most owners have found their unspoiled Chincoteague Pony foals to be even tempered. They tend to think things through. Maybe this is because they are born and indoctrinated in the wild where it's important to think before acting. Still, even the best foal can be ruined by a trainer's quick temper or lack of discipline, so always maintain a level head.

Your foal may move through all the stages of learning at a quick pace or he may need time to reflect on each lesson. Either way, he will still need reinforcement. Each foal learns at his own pace, just as human children do.

CHAPTER SEVEN

Ongoing

Come, Foal, Come

Have you ever seen someone go out to "catch" their horse to go riding? Almost every horseman or horsewoman has seen *that* person with *that* horse, the one that has to be cajoled and coerced with feed buckets and cornering. You do not want to be that horse owner. Begin now to teach your foal to come on command.

Conditioning your foal to come can happen in the stall and in the field. Some people use a clicker. For me, having one more thing to hold is a pain. Instead, use a kissing noise, a specific word or a simple whistle. Standing in front of your foal, make the sound you chose and immediately offer a

It didn't take long for 13-year-old Cwen Cole to teach her 2016 foal, ColtN to come when called. Consistent training will keep your pony coming for many years to come.

treat. From here on out, anytime you make that sound, offer a treat. The foal will relate the sound to the treat and will learn to come as soon as he hears it. Never give the treat until you have made the sound.

We all know it is easy to keep treats in your pocket and give them from your hand. For some foals this works out fine, but for many this can create a new bad habit born of greed – nipping. In their hurry to get the treat the foal nips at the hand that feeds them. So I recommend using a small pan, bowl or bucket to offer a treat. If not always, at least half the time you should use the pan, bowl or bucket. Collapsible bowls are convenient and can fit right into your pocket with the treats.

If your foal nips or begins to crowd you, withhold his treat. Don't reward him until he complies, and with calm, quiet behavior.

If you repeat this training on a regular basis your foal will continue to come to you when he hears the sound that is your signal and you will have taught him a valuable lifetime lesson.

Hoof Picks and Leg Lifts

During your daily sessions outside with your foal there are many things you both can do together. You can groom your foal outside. You can move around him from all sides, touching him all over on a regular basis. Doing this regularly will keep him used to touch on all parts of his body.

Next, begin to teach your foal to lift each leg on command, an important lesson for life. Your foal will need to do this on command when the farrier comes to perform that first-time hoof trim. You want to have him ready to fully cooperate.

Standing at your foal's shoulder and facing his rump, use the thumb and the pointer finger or thumb and pointer *and* index fingers to grasp the leg in the joint just above his chestnut, giving the signal to lift. As you squeeze those fingers on the sides of his leg, lift your foal's hoof. Repeat this several times daily until he learns this is the cue to lift.

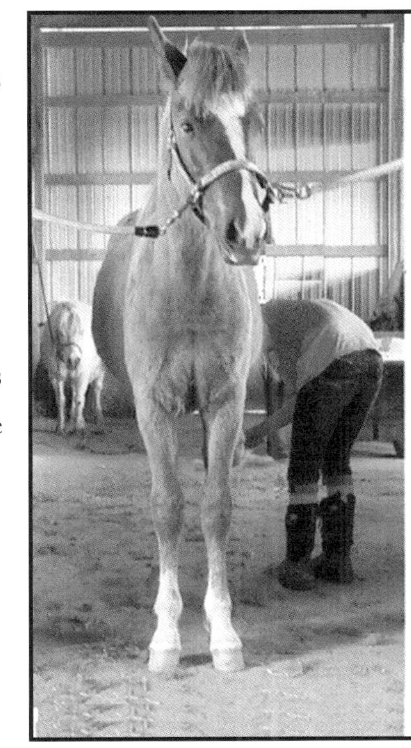

2015 yearling, Suplee's Little Angel stands quietly while 11-year-old Lisa Masley picks her hooves. Lisa said early training was beneficial in teaching Angel to stand quietly for grooming.

Teresa Hemphill said her colt, Twinkie accomplished hauling, haltering, grooming, picking up hooves and allowing touches all over – all in a week and a half. Leading took a bit longer. Chincoteague Ponies are smart little critters!

Vices - Biting

When Janet Mannel's family decided to travel from South Carolina to Virginia for a Pony Penning vacation in 2016, Mannel said they had no plans to purchase a foal.

"We made the plans to see pony penning – we had made it all this way, so we wanted to see it all," Mannel said. "We saw them swim Wednesday morning from Memorial Park and then followed them into town. Our group split up and half of us got to see them parade through the streets of town and the other half of us got to see them just as they entered the carnival ground pens. Unbeknownst to me, my husband and daughter, watched them enter the pens and picked out foals that they wanted."

And Mannel said she wasn't surprised to learn her husband had set up chairs for the sale because he loves auctions in general. Then the auction began.

"I remember the announcer made a particular appeal to fathers in the crowd who may consider purchasing a foal to take home for their child," Mannel said. "Then, my husband, leaning against the chain link fence in front of the foal corrals, gave the slight hand raise after a few bids on foal number one. I couldn't believe it. I knew we came to watch, but I didn't know we came to bid. And to win!"

When they realized he had won the bid, Mannel said her almost 8 year old daughter, Petra- who had been taking riding lessons for months - jumped into his arms and hugged him. It was a moment she said she will never forget.

The Mannel family had a cute three stall barn at home with only a few goats and chickens inside. So, they took home their beautiful chestnut foal with a unique stripe on the nose, shaped just like a paintbrush.

The colt -out the Chincoteague mare, Daisey and by the stallion named Phantom Mist – was named Phantom's Southern Son and nicknamed, Toby.

Mannel had grown up showing horses and reading all the Misty books, so even though getting Toby was a dream come true, she said she is not 100% sure the family was ready for a foal. It wasn't long until the foal developed a habit of biting, a vice Mannel blames herself for, but is determined to correct.

"Nipping leads to biting and I didn't correct it and am regretting it, Now I am trying to backtrack and admonish him whenever he attempts it and in general keep his head out of my space," she said.

Mannel is determined. She said Toby leads, stands for grooming and for the farrier and has a sweet personality.

Petra Mannel and her 2016 colt, Phantom's Southern Son, who has been nicknamed, Toby. Petra and her mom have been working on Toby's vices.

"He is a very playful pony - he loves his jolly ball that he received as a gift for Christmas. I had lots of advice given to me and have done lots of reading and watching training videos, but only until I made mistakes and have reflected on them do I really see how I will do things differently in the future," Mannel said.

Vices that seem minor when a foal is young become major as the horse grows, so – like Mannel – you'll need to work on correction methods while your foal is small.

Twelve-year-old Lisa Masly of New Jersey has worked with horses since she could walk. She shows actively with her 4-H Club, but raising her own Chincoteague Pony foal provided a new experience. Her dedication to training has given her yearling, Angel impeccable ground manners and helped her in overcoming a nagging nipping problem.

"The most important thing about working with your foal is to always end on a good note," Lisa said. "It doesn't matter what you're doing - always end on a good note."

According to Lisa, those last moments of training are what the foal remembers and will affect how they approach the next training session.

Lisa said, "Discipline is very important when it comes to nipping, kicking and running away. Nipping is a very hard habit to break."

She's right. Biting is one of the most dangerous habits a horse can develop. A horse who bites is hard to escape. I once worked at a racing stable where one of the horses had a massive biting problem. Anyone walking past the stall was a target for this unlikable stud, whose strike seemed quicker than a rattlesnake. We workers often drew straws to see who had to clean his stall. Most of us carried bruises on our upper arms at some point during our time on the farm.

Breaking a biter's bad habit is much harder than preventing it before it begins. That's why I am so hugely against hand feeding.

There are several approaches to biting. Trainer, Wendy Hilton, in an article on www.infohorse.com advises taking the nose of a mouthy horse in your hands and rubbing it. She said, "Don't rub so hard that you hurt him. The idea is to be gentle but persistent."

Hilton said the horse will eventually take his head away. She said to repeat this whenever he brings his head and mouth back again.

World renowned trainer, John Lyons uses the three second rule. You have three seconds to respond to a horse's bite, so act fast. Let him know that you are NOT going to put up with his dangerous biting behavior. A hard open handed slap will get his attention and he will remember. It's about cause and effect – He bit and pain his was the immediate effect. Lyons says the hit should NEVER be on the head, never be more than once, and never be hard enough to harm.

Remember that one hard slap is never as heavy as the reception of teeth or hooves he would receive from his dam or other herd members in the wild and may protect him from a future of moving from auction barn to auction barn and owner to owner, perhaps ending up in wretched conditions or on a slaughter truck. No one likes or keeps a biter.

Lisa Masly said her foal nipped twice, a behavior Lisa nipped in the bud, using a different method that she said worked.

"If your foal nips, you back her up right away. Backing up is the best discipline because you're making them do something they don't want to do - but they have to do it," Lisa said.

Whatever method you use to curb a biting habit make sure you are always consistent. Don't switch from one method to another. Stick to your goal of consistency.

Another form of biting happens when a horse develops a habit of reaching out over a stall door to attempt to bite those who pass by. This type of biting is usually due to boredom and indicates your pony needs more time outside the stall in an area where he can run, kick up his heels and activate his mind.

If outside time is limited due to weather or other unpredictable causes, try a Jolly Ball or hanging ball or another one of the myriad of stall toys available for purchase. The hanging Likit toy has two spaces for treats, so offer flavor options. Your pony has to work at the toy to gain access to the treat. Find a way to take your pony's mind off biting, pawing and other poor behaviors by occupying his mind and alleviating boredom.

Vices: Kicking

Kicking is a natural thing for a horse in the wild, but when that kick is aimed at a human it becomes a dangerous habit. A tiny foal's kick may be seen as just an irritant, but when not addressed it will become the kick of a 1,000 - pound animal and serious injuries may result.

There are many reasons horses kick. They kick at biting flies and mosquitoes around the neck, legs and torso. They stamp or kick at tickly weeds and at each other in the field but these are usually not powerful kicks. One symptom of colic may be kicking at the belly. That's a kick you need to pay attention too. Horses use both hind legs to kick at predators or at other aggressive horses. Those are more serious defensive kicks.

As they age, a horse may develop a kicking habit when saddled up, a cow-kick- most likely developed when someone hurt them during the saddling process. Show horses who kick must wear a red ribbon on their tail to warn other riders that the back end of this horse is dangerous.

The best way to prevent kicking is to address the habit during the formative years, while your Chincoteague Pony is still a foal.

Lisa Masly uses the same method with kicking as she does with biting.

"If you get kicked by your pony, calm her down and make her back up," Lisa said. "Just three steps is okay."

Lisa's method works because most horses do not like to back up toward something they cannot see. Being forced to do something he dislikes as a result of his kicking behavior makes your foal think twice before kicking again.

A horse may also kick when it is startled. To prevent this, make sure you speak to your horse and touch his rump as you come around. Let him know where you are in relationship to his body at all times.

Most horses offer some sort of sign that they are going to kick before they actually do it, so keep an eye on your foal's body language. If he pins his ears back, shifts his weight unpredictably or gets a wary look in his eye, beware.

For your foal, kicking is a way to establish dominance, but you must always be the dominant herd member, not your foal. Round pen work can help you establish the role of dominance, teaching your foal that the act of kicking will net him a workout. It's a safe way to establish yourself as the leader.

Another form of kicking is stall kicking, which may or may not be accompanied by pawing or digging. This is caused by boredom when kept inside the stall. Attack this behavior by adding more outside time. If that's not possible, try placing a ball or toys in the stall, or provide more roughage. Even better, spend more time inside the stall with your pony.

Cribbing

Cribbing is often mistaken for wood chewing, but the act of cribbing is more about sucking in air than biting wood.. Cribbing happens when a pony bites onto a fixed surface, frequently stall doors, fences, grain bins and the like. He curves his neck and sucks in air. This is usually accompanied by a grunting noise. Cribbing causes a release of endorphins in the pony, and like a drug addiction, the habit of cribbing is hard to break. It not only damages fences and stalls but can cause weight loss, gastric colic, and excessive tooth wear in your pony.

The 2015 filly that Kyra Peter took home with help from the Feather Fund quickly adapted to life with other ponies and remains free of vices.

Cribbing collars can be purchased but before attacking the symptom, tray to attack the cause. Cribbing is linked to boredom and is often seen with horses stalled for long periods of time.

Some ways to help are to offer more pasture time, or to make your pony's stall more interesting with a hanging ball, stall toys or constant access to quality forage. The longer he has been cribbing the harder this addictive behavior is to break.

Cribbing collars prevent your pony from taking in a deep breath, so he no longer gets the feeling or effect he seeks with the cribbing behavior. The collar has to be removed when he is exercising heavily or it can cause suffocation.

Anti-cribbing food supplements can also be added to your pony's feed. There are varied reports on the success of these supplements.

Preventing Vices

Only use a loud voice or open-hand smack when your foal exhibits dangerous behavior like biting or kicking.

If he gets away with dangerous behavior once, he will think he can do it twice and again, and so on. Before you know it you will have an 800 to 1000 pound beast that you fear. Your pony should know that you love him but at the same time he should always know that you are in charge and that you will not allow bad behavior. Hard work and consistent training will help you raise a safe and dependable pony.

Solid training by Feather Fund recipient, Melissa White has helped her turn out a solid pony who has just begun his show career.

Here is Melissa with her Chincoteague Pony, Bonfire.

CHAPTER EIGHT

Desensitization

Desensitization exercises are an important part of developing your growing foal's brain, preparing your future mount to calmly accept scary stuff that may come his way as an adult pony. You can accomplish this by introducing him to many things that may seem scary.

While your foal is young, gain his trust and make him less spooky with a variety of desensitization exercises. Introduce one new thing at a time. Otherwise, it will accomplish the opposite and make him dread his time with you.

Some desensitization exercises include leading your equine over tarps, shaking trash bags nearby, opening umbrellas, loading onto a horse trailer and unloading, spraying fly spray on the body, running clippers nearby, playing radios, allowing him to hear large engines running and getting him used to many assorted sights and sounds.

Desensitization exercises build trust. Each time your foal overcomes something "scary" that you've introduced, they learn that you will not lead them into a dangerous situation and that you can be trusted. These are trust building exercises that also reinforce good ground manners. Familiarize your foal with as many new situations as possible, but only one at a time. Once the pony completely conquers a task, give him pasture time, food, or quiet time before introducing another task.

Reward good behavior with soft strokes, pats and soft praise or with treats in a bucket. Do not get angry or raise your voice if your foal can't complete a task.

Respect your pony and develop rules and consequences that assure that he also respects you. A pony should never work for you out of fear. Love your pony as you want your pony to love you.

Lisa Masly teaching her 2015 Chincoteague Pony, Angel to walk over cavaletti.

Introducing your foal to all sorts of new things as he grows will help desensitize him so that he is less fearful and more accepting of strange things and different settings. Touch him with a feather duster or other safe items. Walk him over tarps, cavaletti, plastic or canvas.

Trisha and Courtney Gagne of New York State said they utilized many desensitization exercises, something they still do today with the now two-year-old gelding they brought home in 2014 with help from the Feather Fund.

"We [have tried] to introduce him to many different things such as tarps and pool noodles," Trisha said of Spirit's training. "We have played "soccer" with a blow-up ball to help get him used to things moving around him. After a while we would kick the ball closer to him and have it run into his legs to let him know it's okay and not to be afraid of it. In another exercise we did, we used a sheet and hung it up. It took Spirit a little longer to do this one but we eventually got him to walk through it and not to be afraid of it touching his face and covering his eyes."

"We did a lot of walking with him in the beginning but also walking in his pen without [a halter or lead rope], calling him over to see if he would walk up to us," Courtney said of early outside training with Spirit." I loved this exercise because it showed us he really enjoyed being with us and I feel it got our bond started."

Courtney said they also played a game they call the Circle Game.

"[This teaches] your horse to move around you," Courtney said, describing how she tapped his butt with a carrot stick to get him to move around her. "Eventually we could just raise the carrot stick and he knew what he needed to do," she said.

Courtney said she and her sister also taught Spirit to pay attention to their body language and she talked about their favorite exercise based on breathing..

"Ease your air [out] loudly while turning your head towards his hind end. This means 'stop'. Just releasing [a little] air means 'calm down' or 'slow down'. This trick or command is one of my favorites and most important since when walking him you can calm him down just by releasing your air."

During the summer months, take your foal with you almost anywhere you travel on foot, so that he can get used to many different settings.

Laura Bagley, of New York State took her 2016 foal, Tug swimming with her in the local creek. When you get them, Chincoteague Pony foals are

Laura Bagley works with her 2016 colt, Tug.

already water babies. They are used to water, but if you don't continue to expose them to water they could become fearful over time, so continue to bring them to water so that years from now - when you want your pony to cross over a creek or swim in the river - they are ready and willing to carry you there.

Hannah Pavlas of Washington State is a big supporter of Clinton Anderson and has used his Natural Horsemanship methods to train her Chincoteague Pony Mincaye (Min-KY-yee). Clinton and other trainers use a training stick with a string that is basically used as an extension of your arm. It allows you to touch any part of a horse anywhere without putting yourself in harm's way while getting them used to objects touching them. A training stick can also be used to guide the back end of the horse while standing in the front.

Training sticks are generally about three feet long and stiffer than lounge whips, driving whips and crops, so those should not be used as substitutes.

"The first time I went to desensitize Mincaye to a stick and string - a tool used by Clinton Anderson and many other Natural Horsemanship trainers - he literally dragged me all over his pasture," Hannah said. "He ran backward and sideways at alarming speed in an attempt to escape…. and this over just a tiny bit of motion from the string! If my memory serves me, I got so tired that after a while I started praying to God to please make Min stop because I didn't know how much longer I could keep up with him!"

Hannah says today you would never know Min was ever so violently reactive to the stick and string.

"I can spank the ground all around him and flick the string all over his body and around his legs. His main concern now tends to be over the fly or mosquito buzzing in rather than the whiz of the string going by his head! The widely used desensitizing method of "approach and retreat" is the horseman's miracle cure for helping horses overcome all manner of odd little phobias! I remember when I could barely rub Min down with a towel without him freaking out. Using approach and retreat, now I can flap plastic bags all over his body, including his head, and he remains calm and quiet."

Hannah, along with many others interviewed for this book, believes that training your own foal deepens the bond, despite challenges that may arise along the way.

"Learning along with my pony has proven to be very challenging, but the rewards are well worth it to me," Hannah said. "I feel that Min and I have a deeper relationship because I am his trainer. This is not to say that it is all smooth going in our relationship! Min is as feisty as he is smart. We've hit a lot of roadblocks, but we've also overcome so much together. Remembering how far we've come is the perfect tonic to help encourage me on when we're struggling with something. Nothing ever starts out looking pretty."

Round Pen Work

World renowned trainers like John Lyons, Clinton Anderson, Ray Hunt, and Pat Parelli all use round pen training techniques.

Hannah Pavlas does round pen work with her 2010 Feather Fund Chincoteague Pony, Mincaye.

If you don't have a round pen, any paddock with a diameter of 50 to 100 feet can work. Round off the corners with bales of hay or barrels. The reason to eliminate corners is to keep the foal from running into a corner.

Put the foal into the round pen and use a rope or a training stick to drive him around the pen. The rope or stick should not be used to strike the foal. It is a method of keeping the foal moving and out of kicking range. While working in the round pen, if the foal stops or kicks, touch him with the stick or move forward quickly to keep him moving. It will be natural instinct for the foal to run around the circumference of the pen.

You can periodically turn your foal in the pen, to run in the opposite direction. Gently keep him moving. If he slows down or stops, step back and see if he comes to you. If he does, take advantage of this time to connect with him. Pet or rub him softly or stroke him with the training stick. If the foal walks away or turns to kick, get him moving again. His only break will be to come toward you in a nonthreatening way. Don't work the foal for more than 15 minutes in a round pen. Any time you or your foal is sweating, you have worked too long. Doing this on a regular basis helps teach your foal that becoming your friend is a good thing.

Lunging

Lunging is a great way to teach your pony to follow commands and to be more aware of you and is also great regular exercise for a horse kept in a smaller pasture. Before starting make sure your pony has perfected leading and handles well. When lunging, you'll be asking your pony to move faster or slower, bend on a circle or move closer to or farther away from you.

During the training stages to lunge, it helps to have someone working with you. An indoor arena, round pen or open space away from other horses or distractions is ideal. You'll need a long lunge line to hook to the halter and a lunge whip, which is never used to hit a horse.

Hook the lunge line to the horse's halter. If someone is helping out, clip on a regular lead rope, too. While your helper stands on the left side in the normal place to lead, you should stay behind the lunge line. Hold the lunge line in your left hand when doing a counter-clockwise circle and the lunge whip in your right hand. Ask your pony to walk and raise the whip.

I prefer clucking the tongue instead of using the word walk, because you can speed up the clucking sound for a trot and even more for the canter, an easy-to-understand command for most horses. Movement of the lunge line in the air or swooshing it, is also a signal to your pony. While you are on the end of the line, your helper will lead - to show your pony what you are asking for. When you ask for the pony to halt, saying "Whoa," you should also lower the lunge whip. Later, your pony will remember and understand what you want when you are at the end of the long line alone.

Sabrina Dobbins lunges her yearling Chincoteague Pony, A Feathers Blessing.

If you don't have a helper, start lunging in small circles and let them get bigger as you go along. That's what Feather Fund pony recipient, Sabrina Dobbins did when she trained her foal, A Feather's Blessing, to lunge.

"I also talk to her a lot when I'm lunging so she knows exactly what I want and knows when she is doing something correctly," Dobbins said.

Make sure you take time to stop, approach your pony and praise him, patting the neck and speaking in reassuring tones as you train. Switch the lunge line, lead rope, and helper to the other side of the horse when you are ready to work with the pony going in the opposite direction.

Like Hannah, Sabrina said she started with free lunging, giving Blessing the opportunity to move in and out as she pleased.

"She typically stayed pretty fair out which made it really easy when I started with a lunge line," Sabrina said.

If your horse is not doing what you ask - is stopping or slowing down without being asked, coming into the middle of the circle to see you, or is bucking and carrying on - you need to stop and begin again. Don't let your pony control the shots or he will learn that he can take charge in any situation.

Remember that a foal or young pony should work for short periods of time, a less strenuous workout. The knees on ponies under age four have not yet closed over, making sharp, quick turns and jumping unsafe.

Chincoteague Pony foal, Tug is now comfortable with being ponied by Laura, who got Tug with help from the Feather Fund.

Lunging a spunky horse before going out on a ride or before more training can give them a chance to work out the kinks so they are less likely to buck and carry on. If lunging is going to be a part of your training routine try to do it on a regular basis, so your pony remembers what you are asking of him.

Ponying

Chincoteague Pony owner, Laura Bagley says when you are training a young foal, you must be careful how you introduce him to new things, but she believes teaching a foal to pony with another horse can be very useful, a good concept for a young foal to learn. She taught her 2016 foal, Tug how to be ponied alongside her American Quarter Horse gelding, Sunny.

"When teaching your foal to be ponied, you need to take your time," Laura advised. "First, you need to make sure that you have a horse that is calm, responds well to your commands, and that gets along well with other horses. You also need a foal that is halter trained and knows how to lead well. The foal must also be acquainted with the horse before you try ponying."

Laura introduced her two ponies over a fence and later in the pasture with handlers nearby.

"After I was certain that they got along well, I would have another handler lead Sunny while I led Tug right by his side to see how they would react," Laura said. She recommended another handler help the first time you pony your foal, too.

"You will need proper equipment in order to pony your foal," she said. "I use a long lead rope for the foal and I rode my horse with a saddle until both horses were well acquainted with the idea. I hold the reins in my left hand and lead Tug along with my right hand. This is why it is a good idea to have a horse that neck-reins. Make sure that you start small, just take a few steps and stop to show the foal what you want and expect of him."

Training sessions should stay short, she advised, about 5-10 minutes. Eventually you will work your way up to doing circles, serpentines, and even trotting, side by side. Like Lisa, Laura said to be sure to always end your training on a good note.

CHAPTER NINE

Before You Can Ride

When you think about the right age a horse should be before you climb aboard, please do NOT look to the racing industry. Most yearlings bred to race do not carry more than 150 pounds and are never trained more than 15 minutes per day, but they are still ridden far too young. The evidence is in the sheer number of horses who break down at a young age.

At age two, a horse is physically old enough to sit on but waiting until age three or four is a wiser decision for several reasons. First, most horses are not emotionally ready until they are at least three. Second, the skeletal structure of a horse will not stop growing until somewhere around six years of age.

If you wisely decide to start riding your Chincoteague Pony between the ages of three or four, jumping and galloping should still take a back seat until age five or six. The spinal joints don't reach full development and strength until five to six years of age and the force of a rider in full gallop can be damaging, as can the centrifugal motion of a horse landing a jump.

When you do start to ride your Chincoteague Pony, remember that bones and joints need regular conditioning. That means working your way slowly upward, starting with walk and trot and continuing with daily workouts. If your workouts slow down, then the pace of what your horse is doing must slow down, too. Whenever you take a break in daily training or riding, you must go back and go over early training work before moving on. With consistent training sessions you can work your way up to cantering and finally a full gallop. Don't attempt jumping until your horse has been conditioned to gallop. Knees are particularly vulnerable in unconditioned horses and ponies.

While you wait for your horse to mature to riding age, here are a few fun tricks you can train him to do. Work in short sessions. Patience, repetition and a sense of humor are important.

Trick Training: Smile

Hannah Pavlas is a big fan or Clinton Anderson and his Down Under training program and she has followed it to a T- from the time she got her Chincoteague Pony foal, Mincaye (Min-KY-yee) in 2010, through today.

"I feel that Min and I have a deeper relationship because I am his trainer," Hannah says. That deeper relationship drove her to teach Mincaye a list of tricks. Each time you train something new you are developing your pony's mind and strengthening the bond you share.

Hannah has taught Mincaye many tricks over the years. She said she used tips from the book "Trickonometry" by renowned trick trainer Carole Fletcher.

In the book, Fletcher says the trainer should stand directly in front of his horse or pony, holding the lead rope. While saying "Smile" let your foal sniff a strange smelling odor (like a cut onion, a lemon or ammonia on a cloth). He should react fairly quickly by curling his lip up and sometimes he will raise his head, too, like a stallion does when scenting a mare.

As soon as your foal curls his lip, reward him with a treat. Repeat these steps over and over until your foal curls his lip up as soon as he sees your hand out and hears the word "Smile".

Chincoteague Pony, Mincaye perfects his smile!

Other trainers have gotten the same result by tickling the inside of the upper lip while saying, "Smile," continuing until the horse does "smile," and then rewarding with a treat. Getting to know your foal will help you know which method is most likely to work for you.

Trick Training: Bow

My daughter, Shannon taught her Chincoteague Pony, Sea Feather to bow when he was a two year old. Since then he has bowed for hundreds of school children and even on Veterans Day at a war memorial in West Virginia.

To teach the bow, you must back your horse up to a fence or a wall, so that he cannot back up any further. Standing on his right side and holding his halter with the right hand and the treat in the left, show him the treat. Put the treat under his belly and through his legs, saying "Bow." Your horse's natural instinct will cause him to stretch his legs out to get his head lower. Reward him with the treat.

1995 Chincoteague Pony, Sea Feather bows.

Repeat the process, but next time, slowly draw the treat backwards toward his mid-belly, all the while saying, "Bow". This will bring him down even further toward the ground.

Each time you say bow and your horse stretches his legs, lowers his head and in effect, bows, he gets a treat. In time, he will associate the bow with the treat and will only need to hear the word.

Even though most foals will bend down and stretch under fences to find greener grass, do make sure your foal's bones have had enough conditioning to perform this trick. Now that Sea Feather is 22 years old, Shannon seldom asks him to bow because his bones are mostly likely not as limber as they once were.

Training: Natural Inclinations

If your horse has a habit that seems peculiar, see if you can use it to your advantage. I did this when training my dog to bow. Every time he wanted to play he would go down on his front legs, butt up, wiggling. I started saying Bow, every time he did this and then rewarding him with a treat. It didn't take long for him to learn how to bow on command.

Think about the things your horse does. Is he a head shaker? You can turn this into "No". Come up with a question that you can ask in front of a group. "Do you want a saddle on your back?" or "Are you going to give me a kiss?" are good ones to start with. Now, every time your foal shakes his head, (while he is shaking) ask the question and then reward him with the treat. Create an association between the action, the question and the treat. Chincoteague Ponies are smart and they catch on quickly.

Trick Training: Hugs

There's nothing better than getting a hug from your horse and it is one of the easier tricks to teach.

Stand on your foal's right side, facing outward. Then, with your right hand, hold a treat out. When he reaches for the treat – and while saying "Hugs!" slowly draw your hand around the front of you and to the opposite side, forcing the foal to wrap his head around you to get the treat. Repeat until he has learned to respond to the word "Hugs!" and to get his treat.

Trick Training: Shake

Every gentleman knows how to shake hands, or hoof to hand! For this one, first teach your horse to raise his leg when you tap his knee or cannon bone with your hand, or lightly with a crop.

Stand beside the leg you want him to give you for "the shake". Gently tap his knee or cannon bone for two or three seconds and say "Shake". Immediately after you stop tapping, reach down and lift his foot, as you would to pick his hoof. Let go of the hoof and give him a treat. After he has begun to lift the leg as soon as you say "Shake", move to his front and tap the leg while standing in front of him. Lift the leg if necessary and reward with a treat.

Practice makes perfect, and the shake is no different than all other exercises, so repeat the process until he has learned to lift his leg as soon as you give him the verbal cue.

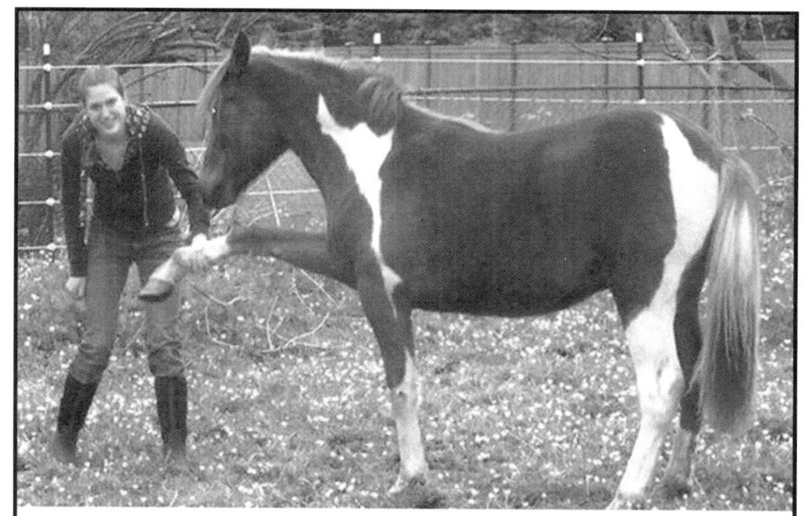

Hannah Pavlas taught her 2011 Chincoteague Pony, Mincaye to shake hands.

Remember to teach tricks in a location that has few distractions. If your equine doesn't "get it" immediately, don't be disappointed. Just return to the trick and further training on another day. Don't push your pony. If he shows any aggression with a trick, stop training immediately and work on basic ground manners again. There have been incidences of striking or pawing associated with teaching the handshake trick too quickly, so proceed with caution.

Trick Training: Standing on a Stool:

Every Chincoteague Pony owner wants to teach their foal to stand on a stool, just like Misty did! We taught our 1995 colt, Sea Feather to stand on a stool as a young foal and he is still doing it as a 23 year old gelding.

My husband, Dan built the stool we used, making it about a foot high, with a foot square top and a 16" square on the bottom. He painted the top with textured paint (made with sand in it) to prevent the pony's hooves from sliding off the top.

Although many other types of stools have been used, it is most important to be sure your stool is sturdy enough that it won't break or collapse and that the top is skid proof, so they don't slide off the stool. It only takes one accident to take away a pony's confidence and make him shy away from a trick.

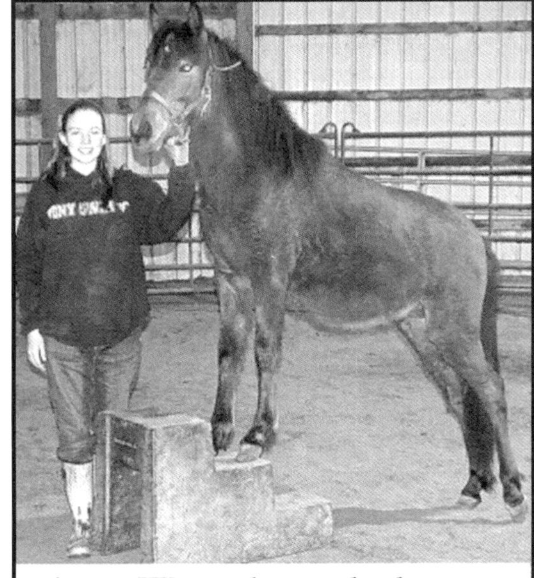

Amy Wetzel taught her 2011 Chincoteague Pony Buckeye to stand on a stool.

Amy Wetzel spoke about training her Chincoteague Pony, Babe's Buckeye to stand on a stool.

"Once Buckeye was desensitized [to] the stool and was willing to walk up to it I then began tapping the back of his knee while saying the word, "*Up*," Amy said. "The first couple times I had to place his leg [on the stool] and follow up with lots of praise so he was aware of what I wanted. He quickly caught on and then I would ask for the other leg."

Amy said it didn't take long for her to be able to say *"Up"* and tap the leg and see him step right up.

"I found that this also helped with teaching him to trailer load," Amy shared, "because he was already aware of the step up que and I would use it when he walked in."

Trick Training: Teaching a Foal to Lie Down

Lying Down - Method #1

In a blog post in the *Performance Horse Digest,* Western trainer Ken McNabb recommended teaching your horse to lie down.

"I teach this exercise because it is a great way to build your horse's trust," McNabb wrote. "When he lies down, he is putting all of his trust in you to look out for his safety."

It is helpful to teach your foal, or horse, to bow before starting this trick if you are using this method of training. Make sure there is room for the foal to move about, before starting, so he doesn't get a leg stuck under a fence or get backed up against a wall or stall door. Outside is best. Your foal needs to be quiet and calm to teach this trick, so if he is still skittish, go back to groundwork and desensitization before you try this one.

Halter your foal before you begin training. Then, wrap a soft, cotton lead rope around one front leg, just above the hoof. Throw the rest of the rope

This sketch shows the path the rope should take around the horse, when you're teaching your pony to lie down.

under his belly and to the opposite side. Wrap it over his back, under his belly and to the opposite side. Then wrap it over his back, coming back to the side the where you have the rope tied to his leg.

Move to the side of the horse where the hoof is tied. Ask your horse to bow while putting pressure on the rope. Ideally, he should go down on one knee. Continue to apply pressure while saying, "Down, or whatever verbal cue you've chosen. As you continue to apply pressure he will slowly lie down. Do not rush him, pull too hard, or do anything that would harm your horse. Never yell or show impatience.

Immediately, after he is down, pat his neck, praise him and shower him with affection. Slowly move to his side and continue to pet his belly and praise him.

Afterward, take his halter and ask him to stand. Let him take his time and when he is up again continue to shower him with praise. Do not repeat this trick over and over in one day or you will burn him out. This is a trick that takes a lot of energy for the horse to complete, and you do not want to burn him out. Repeat it the next day or at least several times in a week to be sure he gets it. And when he does, you will no longer need the rope, only the verbal cue.

<u>Lying Down - Method # 2:</u>

"Teaching your horse to calmly and obediently lie down for you can have many benefits," said 2016 Feather Fund foal recipient, Laura Bagley. "It teaches your horse to trust you, can build your bond, and shows your dominance over your horse. When I taught my Chincoteague Pony, Tug, to lie down, I made sure that I took my time to teach him so that I did not rush him so that he would stay calm."

Laura said she used her own method to teach her foal this trick, and she recommended those who teach this trick do it in a soft area.

"When I taught Tug to lie down, I used his normal halter and lead rope," Laura said. "Then I stood on his left side by his shoulder and asked him to pick up his left front hoof. When he picked it up, I held it at the knee and slowly lowered his knee to the ground so that he was on his left knee with his right leg extended in front of him. I made sure that I had a good hold on his halter as I did this so that he would stay steady."

Laura Bagley taught her 2016 Feather Fund foal, Tug to lay down on command.

Laura said the first time she tried this trick, Tug would try to get up or he would struggle.

"I had to repeat this step a lot of times before Tug was used to the idea of going down on one knee. When I was able to get him on one knee without any struggles, I tipped his head toward his left side - toward me. This [brought] the right side of his neck closer to the ground. After holding his head there, it did not take Tug long to realize that if he rolled over onto his right side he could escape the pressure."

Laura said the trick took several tries, but once he realized what she was asking, he became a quick learner.

Trick Training: Spanish Walk

Hannah Pavlas says one of the more difficult tricks she has taught Mincaye is the Spanish Walk, an intricate dance of sorts in which the horse or pony lifts his legs, "Right, left, right, left" on command.

"We began learning the Spanish Walk," Hannah recalled, "but when I started focusing more on groundwork and later [on] riding exercises, trick training got put on the back burner."

Hannah said she has plans to master the Spanish Walk in the months to come, and though it's not perfected they have made progress.

"I referred to Suzanne Fargher's book "In A Whisper" to help me teach Min the beginnings of the Spanish Walk," Hannah said. "Since I had already taught Min to shake hands, it was pretty easy to get him to understand to lift a right or left leg on command when I pointed at it and gave him a voice cue."

Hannah then added a new challenge - teaching Mincaye to alternate lifting a right or left leg while she stood beside him, instead of in front of him.

"From there, I began asking him to take a step forward after each leg lift, and that was our Spanish Walk," Hannah said. "Min wasn't solid enough at consistently stepping and raising his legs high enough for me to add it to our list of learned tricks."

Even so, according to Hannah, months later when she was riding she experimented to see if he would lift each foreleg while she was on his back and at a standstill. And he did, proving how smart our little Chincoteague Ponies really are!

Feather Fund recipient, Hannah Pavlas taught her 2011 Chincoteague Pony, Mincaye to do the Spanish Walk.

Chincoteague Ponies are smart and sensible and frequently they are quick to learn. Your little wild foal has untapped potential. Enjoy every minute you spend with him. Then, watch him excel!

CHAPTER TEN

Odds and Ends

Just think, your baby started out as a tiny foal born on a wind-battered wild island with a herd for a family. Now *you* are his family. And in just a few more years he will be the full-grown pony of your dreams. You'll be starting to saddle train, trick train or train to pull a cart. You may choose to pursue riding English, or maybe Western. Your pony may be more suited to dressage, stadium jumping, cross country competitions, barrel racing, Western Pleasure, gymkhana, endurance competitions or maybe some other exciting avenue. While moving on to that may seem like the *most exciting* time you and your Chincoteague Pony will spend together, these early years are certainly the *most important* ones. These are the years that you lay the strong foundation you need - with good health care and feeding, basic care and training. These are the years you learn the most about each other and develop a deep bond that will carry you into the future. Your foal is finding out that you and he are teammates who can trust and rely on each other - for many years to come.

How tall will he be?

Are you wondering how tall your Chincoteague Pony foal will be when he is full grown? Here's how you can get a ballpark figure. Measure from the middle of the knee to the coronet band (the top of the hoof). However many inches that measurement is, that is approximately how many hands tall your pony will be when he reaches full maturity. This test doesn't always work, but it is fairly accurate.

Fun Facts

- Did you know that a horse's brain is the size of a walnut? Can you imagine being that smart with such a small brain? They must use it all.
- Did you know that sixteen muscles inside a horse's ear allow him to rotate the ear 180 degrees?
- Did you know that horses can sleep standing up or lying down?
- Did you know that George Washington had a Chincoteague Pony named Chinky? It is said that he rode his Chincoteague Pony over 140 miles, from Mount Vernon to Williamsburg, Virginia.
- Did you know that horses cannot vomit? That's why choking is of particular concern.
- Horses have the largest eye of any animal that lives on land.
- There are over 200 breeds of horses in the world.
- The oldest horse on record was a horse named Old Billy in Great Britain. He lived 62 years.
- And how about this - Male horses have 40 teeth but females only have 36.

Finding Chincoteague Pony Lovers Online

Raising your own foal will be an experience to remember. Bonding, growing together and seeing all the steps of progress makes your adventure even more rewarding. And sharing it with others who love Chincoteague Ponies makes it fun. There will be times over the years that you will have questions that only another Chincoteague Pony owner can answer.

Find other CP owners online where they are nearly always ready to share experiences, give advice or lend a hand. Look for the *I Love Chincoteague Ponies* Facebook page, a community of over 4,500 Chincoteague Pony owners and Chincoteague Pony lovers. If you are looking to contribute to a fund to purchase a buyback pony who will live on the island forever, look for the group: *The Chincoteague Legacy Group: Friends of the Chincoteague Ponies.* In addition, YouTube has numerous training videos.

Those interested in the Feather Fund can learn more at www.featherfund.org or www.featherfund.net or find them on Facebook.

Those interested in the Chincoteague Pony Rescue can learn more at: www.chincoteagueponyrescue.org or find them on Facebook.

For information on Pony Penning and other events by the Chincoteague Volunteer Fire Company, find them on Facebook or learn more on their website at: http://cvfc3.com

Also visit the island's Chamber of Commerce at: www.chincoteaguechamber.com

In Memory of
SurferDude

Afterward

First, I'd like to congratulate you on your new foal! As Marguerite Henry once said of these ponies - you have purchased a piece of the wind and the sky - but you've also purchased a sturdy, hardy foal bred to survive.

This book is intended to help you start the bonding and training process with your new foal. I've covered suggested feeding, housing, health care and ground manner training for the formative years with the hope that, with patience and daily interaction your foal will develop the calm attitude needed to make him more receptive in his later years when you undertake saddle training, cart training and more.

Without good care and basic ground manners in the formative years, training in later years can become a huge undertaking. These basic foal-start suggestions should make additional training a breeze.

Much appreciation goes out to the many sources cited in this book including (but not limited to) Deb Ober of the Chincoteague Pony Rescue, Veterinarians – Allison Dotzel, and Alison Meyer, Steve and Darcy Cole of DSC Photography for their reports, Shannon Meyers for proof-reading the book, numerous Feather Fund children, foal owners, horse trainers and members of the Chincoteague Pony community at large. And as always, I am grateful to the Chincoteague Volunteer Fire Company for caring for these ponies and keeping the breed alive. Thank you also, to everyone who shared their pony story openly so that others may benefit.

Lois Szymanski

Competing in dressage, here is Summer Barrick and the 2005 Chincoteague Pony she took home, with help from the Feather Fund. Summer now helps other foal and pony owners, operating her own training business, called *Within Stride Training, LLC.*

INDEX

Sabrina Dobbins showed her yearling, A Feather's Blessing in classes while still young, a fine way to introduce your foal to a world beyond your barn and farm gates.